By Alan Dugan

POEMS 4

POEMS 4

by ALAN DUGAN

An Atlantic Monthly Press Book

LITTLE, BROWN AND COMPANY • BOSTON • TORONTO

FIRST EDITION

Library of Congress Cataloging in Publication Data

Dugan, Alan.
  Poems 4.

  "An Atlantic Monthly Press book."
  I. Title.
PS3554.U33P62   811'.5'4   73-19676
ISBN 0-316-19470-0
ISBN 0-316-19471-9 (pbk.)

ATLANTIC–LITTLE, BROWN BOOKS
ARE PUBLISHED BY
LITTLE, BROWN AND COMPANY
IN ASSOCIATION WITH
THE ATLANTIC MONTHLY PRESS

Published simultaneously in Canada
by Little, Brown & Company (Canada) Limited

PRINTED IN THE UNITED STATES OF AMERICA

For Judy

Some of these poems have been previously published by *Arion's Dolphin, Harper's Magazine, Madrona, Partisan Review, Poetry* ("Stentor and Mourning"), *Shankpainter, The American Poetry Review* ("For a Lost Girl" and Untitled Poem in Two Parts: I. "When I woke up . . ."; II. "There are effects . . ."), *The Atlantic* (On Leaving Town," "On Looking for Models," "On Being Easy in the Ritual of Separation"), and *The Columbia Forum.*

Table of Contents

POEMS 4

I. BUSINESS JACOB, THE ANGEL WRESTLER

Not to avoid him but
to try him rightly armed
is why I go around

sweating with business while
an "I" sits sound asleep
wisely in full awares.

It waits for a touch at night,
touching its terrors, to
reply: "Here is your man,

Angel: wrestle him fed,
housed by the working day,
and clothed in currency,"

but only hears a voice
laughing and going away,
saying, "No thanks,

I don't fight punks."

II. COMMENT ON "BUSINESS JACOB, THE ANGEL WRESTLER"

You can't win, you can't draw,
sometimes you can't even lose,
but even to train up to such a fight
is Victory. That man is lucky who
has even had his challenge listened to:
he can go out at night sometimes
and play around with the beasts,
and not get locked indoors to sleep
with the women, children, and slaves,
dreaming: "Isn't there something else
that I should do or die? What
have I got to lose except securities?"

MORNING AT SPEED PRODUCTS

The operators stood around the cold shop
and coughed at dirty morning jokes about
the mysteries of family life behind
them and the certainty of work ahead.
Then, when the bell rang, they each resolved,
"No man should work, but be,"
and went to put their wrists inside
the safety handcuffs of machines.
Each man was doing life in dreams
for wages, some shit's profits, and his own
payment on his dreamed family plan.

PRAYER

God, I need a job because I need money.
Here the world is, enjoyable with whiskey,
women, ultimate weapons, and class!
But if I have no money, then my wife
gets mad at me, I can't drink well,
the armed oppress me, and no boss
pays me money. But when I work,
Oh I get paid!, the police are courteous,
and I can have a drink and breathe air.
I feel classy. I am where the arms are.
The wife is wife in deed. The world
is interesting!, except I have to be
indoors all day and take shit, and make
weapons to kill outsiders with. I miss
the air and smell that paid work stinks
when done for someone else's profit, so I quit,
enjoy a few flush days in air, drunk, then
I need a job again. I'm caught in a steel cycle.

SAINT MONDAY

Without a raincoat
I can not go out
looking for work,
so I sit in the kitchen
looking at old snapshots:

the dead at parties
or at the beach,
you nude at three
reading the New York Times!
Love, it is winter again:

the summer broke us.
I might find work
before next Sunday
so we can take a stroll
with money in cold weather.

ON A DISPOSSESS PRECEPT. I

———————

"We are being torn down.
Everything must go," the sign
in the downstairs window read.
They have the laws and pries
on their side; we have
dear rubbish from the year
one. It will be pushed away
in baby carriages at gun-
point to a relocation elsewhere,
out in the dumps by The Kills.

ON A DISPOSSESS PRECEPT. II

———————

There are rats disguised
in baby-bonnets in
your baby carriages, mothers,
so don't suckle: save your teats
for a following generation.
Where have all your babies gone?
To join the revolution. They won't last.

DEFENDANT

Someone kicked him so he limped.
Someone hit him and his flinch
shriveled his spine. He crawled to court
in answer to an ad that read:
"Justice, to be done, demands
some practice on whoever comes
in any way bent to her hand."

UNTITLED POEM

The city is empty, like a dangerous area,
except for me. One side of the street
is light: that's moonlight: that's the moon.
If I should meet a page of newsprint
flopping in the gutter like a stranded fish,
who else is there to say which one of us
is the noisier alien of this street.

ON LEAVING TOWN

This must be a bad dream. We will wake up
tomorrow naked in the prior garden, each
entwined in his particular love. We will
get up to natural water, fruits, and what?,
a gambol with the lions? Nonsense. This
is petrified obsession, perfect in tautology,
visible in the smoke, the layout of the streets,
and prison buildings. The city has put on
glass armor in rock war against its death,
which is internal. It rides out radiate
on country roads to ride down enemy foliage.
Why? There's nothing left in it to kill
except its people, and they look thoroughly every way —
left, right, front, back, up, down, and in —
before they cross another, or its streets. Such animals,
joyful of desolate beauties, they are so tough, the live ones,
that they stand around like Easter Island statues of survival won
by casual struggle, proud of their tension or their craft.
Oh I reject the dream but not the city. I
have loved its life and left it and I am
a better animal for having learned its ways;
but it is not enough to be a captive animal,
social in town. Escaped emotions: boredom and fear.

PASSING THROUGH THE BANFORD TOLLS

Proceeding sidewise by inattention I arrive
unknowingly at an unsought destination
and pass it by wondering: what next?

ON VOYAGE

Always getting ready to go out
but never leaving, I looked out
at the developments of the day
from morning up to noon and down
to afternoon and, after that,
night. "To take off," I said,
"always to leave, to begin again,"
but I stayed in my paces and room
always getting ready to go out
but never leaving. Ah how I worked
my youth away to send word out
to the day about my situation. Then
it sent back steamship tickets and
a hammer of images forged by deaths,
the idea of death, and cash, the savior.
"I have broken through," I said
to the window for the last time,
and walked out on to the ocean and
Europe for a closer view of home.

HEART ATTACK IN BAD AIR,

so stumble, heart, under the weight
of heavy air and loss of teeth,
hair, eyes, veins, arteries, balls and all,
plus living memory. Ah let them all
go bad or gone and grin the grin
of the infarcted man. What's left
of positive identity except
the papers in the wallet in between
the heart and hand the cops find?
Oh I had wanted something else
besides due bills, a passive position
under the state and on the sidewalk
under circling red lights in yellow air
while heaving prayers to the long green.
When someone steps on my eyeglasses,
however, I find I do not have to care.

UNTITLED POEM

Let them take to the air before
it leaves, and afterwards, to space.
This rock is alternately wet or dry,
iced or dusted on the surface, hot
at heart, and withering. They,
they say, are going to the stars
in office, seated at a desk
in uniforms of solid air
and senseless, but for instruments.
I might be blind naked, but I know
the star of earth is literally internal.

The independent subway of the mind
must go beneath the crust and beds
or rivers, lovers, and the dead
to hunt, as end, means, and cause,
the star they say they're flying for,
straitjacketed in padded cells inside
a weapon, watching face-mask television.

ON THE LIQUIDATION OF ZOOLOGY

We put the mountains in the valleys,
the oceans in the deserts,
and paved the world flat.
The botanical trash was burned,
and life put in its place: zoos.
In this way we cleaned up
in honor of the flat out
continuity of the green glass sea
and walked on it like Christ
in horror of the bad old days
when any kind of life ran wild
and men did as they pleased.

RISING IN FALL,

the mushrooms feel like stiff pricks made of rot.
Oh spreading glans, what
a botanical striving to butt
hogberry branches and leaves apart
to rise to fuck the sky so fast,
six inches in, up IT, with dirt
on top of each umbrella ribbed beneath,
in one night after rain. Stars,
there is life down here in the dark.
It wants you, upward, but not much.
The mushrooms die so fast
in their external manifestations that
their maggots working to be flies
make moving liquid of their blackening heads.
Oh you can see them falling downward for a week
to dirt — that's when they really live —
and then the flies take off.
How high do they get to sting us?
Not high. It's ridiculous. I ask
a woman, "Do you get the point
of all this pointless action?"
She answers, "Naturally. Yes. Idiot."

ON LOOKING FOR MODELS

The trees in time
have something else to do
besides their treeing. What is it.
I'm a starving to death
man myself, and thirsty, thirsty
by their fountains but I cannot drink
their mud and sunlight to be whole.
I do not understand these presences
that drink for months
in the dirt, eat light,
and then fast dry in the cold;
they stand it out somehow,
and how, the Botanists will tell me.
It is the "something else" that bothers
me, so I often go back to the forests.

PORTRAIT IN THE FORM OF AN
EXTENDED CONCEIT

A coal mine is a hollow tree
upside down for miners
every spring. The leaves,
whose edge is sometimes coal,
eat dirt for natural gas,
but the roots breathe air.

"Hit bottom and find it
rock to build on," it is said.
He dug where miners
wish away their lives
for daylight, pitted in the leaf.
They surface for a night of it,
high in the airy roots
and wash the naked smuts away.

Not him. He said. I quote:
"I cut the last step down
to a permanent landing, praying
for foundation in the depths,
but after each step down,
after the last, I have the shock
of unexpected falls in sliding shale."

Architects in earth
turned outside-in
despise their galleries:
they dream of bulk,
not holes. They want
to build in rock
what others float on surfaces,

and sap their plans
with soundings. Visibly,
he looked like slag-heaps
and a bitter tipple,
a machine plus waste
whose act is out of sight.

Strict as a meander,
unforethoughtout,
his sculpture of neglect
is deadly hollow underground.
Oh it redeems his curse of self
and tool-sounds down the shaft
with private profit, luxuries,
since an efficiency
for groundless ends
can tool another use:
the roots are upwards, but
some place is earned below
by self-lit slaves of his company.

RESOLUTION OF HESITANCIES

Over-elaboration of scaffolding
is fool's construction since the work
itself is always unbegun.
I could top out on my high plans
and fly the flag with the device
"Grief for lost chances" over all
preparation, but at my age and without
reasons or children, I go to work
to lay the first stone, no more, no less,
and hollow of all contents and effects,
to be the headstone of a triumph carved:

"Cornerstone, I $\left\{ \begin{array}{l} \text{have} \\ \text{might} \end{array} \right\}$ come through."

THE DARK TOWER

After George Gordon, Lord
Byron, the revolutionary
democrat and lover of
Greece, 1788–1824.

The swamp around the tower was alive
with animals and was an animal itself.
Everybody looked at everybody; things
felt out things until it was Resolved:
Who is the strongest. Then the animals
attacked, ran, or fawned; the swamp
held up its tracks or let them drop.
The old black keep which I approached
past fawning animals on solid bog
was no more awful than a broken tooth
except for the man who has it. I knocked
to test his nerve and stake my claim
to what is mine by nature, his by name.

UNTITLED POEM

I never saw any point
to life because I suffered
all the time, but now
that I am happy or bored
for whole days out of pain
I regret my past inactions.
Oh I could do nothing else.

I am almost too old
to learn about human life
but I try to, I
watch it curiously and try
to imitate its better processes.
So: First pleasures after hard times,
Hello in time for goodbye.

UNTITLED POEM

Speciously individual
like a solid piece of spit
floating in a cuspidor
I dream of free bravery
but am a social being.
I should do something
to get out of here
but float around in the culture
wondering what it will grow.

ON BEING EASY IN THE RITUAL OF SEPARATION

Morning: from sleep to confusion.
Celebration of relevant anodynes.
Gymnastic pacing. Elimination. EAT.
Read the paper: politics: interesting:
personal intervention ineffective from
Marxist-Leninist point of view.
Go to work. Work. COME HOME.
Moment of clarity: Meet god.
Conversation as to the relation
between being and becoming.
Some relation. Whiskey. EASY.
Read. Sleep before morning. EAT.
MAKE MONEY. MAKE SONS. DIE.

Thanks for the moment before dreams.
Moment of clarity, relations,
work, conversation, god,
whiskey, sleep, thanks, EASY.

ABOUT THE PSEUDO ST. DIONYSIUS

For him the cosmos was a pearl, hell
contagious at its center, and around it
a burnt-out crust of earth
cooled but not cured by wild salt water.
Then, set as seals against this ill,
in laminated spheres in turning spheres,
rose heavens of pure shifting light.
However, he despised such jewelry,
and through the ninefold veils of shells
that censored him from love, he prayed
to burst like trees from seeds,
slowly in final Spring, and reach the heart
of the empyrean self-curing oyster-god
who should be everywhere beyond his search,
holding his flaw in brilliant quarantine.

UNTITLED POEM IN TWO PARTS

I

When I woke up with my head in the fireplace
I saw the sky up the chimney. "No clouds",
I thought. "Good god day, what did I do
last night to wake up in these ashes fortunately cold?"

Nerves, nerves, the sky is coming in to land
but I don't care. What I can't stand is conversation,
so I rape myself in retrospect and have a day.

II

There are effects
of mine all over. What
I did I'll never know
but should retrieve
my acts by their
debris, right? There are:
clothes on the stairs,
a broken window, trash
cans in the flower-bed,
a woman singing "Hi
honey", and what else?
I must have left
by the broken window or

[27]

I broke it with her head
and then came back.

Echoes of shouts on the air
are proofs of another self:
I walk around to find
it. Oh I don't know
what happened but I wish
I did because I did it,
right? Wrong. Is
everything all right?
Yes. No. Rest in the mystery.
Begin a new day.

UNTITLED POEM

Two shots down and I'm exalted,
so I have the choice: do I give out
the passion of the day to whiskey, arts and crafts,
and lose tomorrow's to the shakes and nausea,
or do I be a joiner with the bourgeoisie
and cool it, feed, do labor, and make sleep?
Ah how I envy my iron-gut youth
when I could drink and talk all night
and get to work next morning, work the day,
and come home to a woman saying honey.

LOVE SONG: CLASS ANALYSIS

I was raised in the suburbs where spite is the child of love,
and mortgagors worked out a doubted safety with their lives.
I heard them whisper of the threats implicit in an alien smile,
so it's no wonder that I ran away from such a patrimony
in pursuit of alien smiles, and found a foreign girl to love,
immigrant to my hate. I felt that she could help
me to come through to love beyond that class of property,
but I am what I am by birthright, she is no longer foreign.

ON A PROFESSIONAL COUPLE IN A SIDE-SHOW

She is the knife-thrower's lady:
around her outline
there is a rage of knives.
Unharmed, he hopes, inside,
she is love's engine
of dark business
and the target of design.

What does she think of this?
The same, reversed: money is money
and spangled tights.
Those whistling knives of his
are kitchened at night.

FAMILY STATEMENTS

Wife: We'll gather all the people together
       and build the castle, layer on layer.

Husband: It's a hard birth,
                a short life,
            and death forever,
              so why work?

Daughter: Yes
               and no
            and maybe so
       and everywhere all over.

COP-SHOOTING: ON A NEWSPAPER PHOTOGRAPH

She just shot him, in the Daily News,
and who can blame her? He,
a sitting cop, and she, a good,
big-hearted woman with a noble flaw:
fury. Cops who have to take their guns
home should see to this: it can
be murder. If the service of the gun
had not been home as a persuader, she
would still be private in her rages, not
as public as that bully Akilles, who,
when shown the metals of good arms,
"at once was moved to use them."

UNTITLED POEM

I've promised that I will not care about things,
persons, or myself, but I do. For example:
my house looks like a set for a New England tragedy
but it isn't. Outside it looks like a dump.
What it's like inside I'm too arrogant to describe
although we're happy for whole moments at a time
during this "life is pain" phenomenon.
Nevertheless my objects, loves and self
interfere with my own being. We should,
me and my wife, burn all this down
and start again possessionless toward death
and not together, which is nonsense. Loves,
marriages, families are stultifying in
accumulations of debris of love and artifacts.
Let it all go, as it will, upwards in the fire after death.

ON BEING A HOUSEHOLDER

I live inside of a machine
or machines. Every time one
goes off another starts. Why
don't I go outside and sleep
on the ground. It is because
I'm scared of the open night
and stars looking down at me
as God's eyes, full of questions;
and when I do sleep out alone
I wake up soaking wet
with the dew-fall and am
being snuffed at by a female fox
who stinks from being skunked.
Also there are carrion insects
climbing my private parts. Therefore
I would find shelter in houses,
rented or owned. Anything that money
can build or buy is better than
the nothing of the sky at night,
the stars being the visible past.

UNTITLED POEM

Once on the beach at night I heard the waves
of all drowned sailors organized into a plot
to kill me. They shouted "Come", or "Om",
in a collective voice of combers. I said "No",
though tempted, "not for a while", and left.
They have been liquidated on the whet-wheel of time
or have been ground between the moon's wheel above them
and the earth's wheel beneath. They are what happens to sand
once the sand is ground away. They have become
the lubrication of the process. So how could they say "Come",
or "Om"? They're nothing. They are life's come to death
in our mother, the ocean; so I do not want to join them.

UNTITLED POEM

Who can abide whom or what? That's
the problem of my harbor where
the goddess Liberty holds up her green
pistachio ice cream cone to all
comers and children: they have
to go up underneath her skirts
to reach the windows in her diadem
to be her living jewels. They stare out
as strangers at their city and her harbor.
They think — they're all the brains she has! —
"It's been a hard climb up here but we paid
to be allowed to, so we'll look around and leave
our named hearts dated on her vaginal walls,
and leave because it's easier going down."
They don't take her, Emma Lazarus, they don't
take Liberty, although you said she says she gives.

UNTITLED POEM

I'm in the house because
the killed dog has escaped
and barks all day
on the sand hills around us.
(The hunters are out in red
turncoats: the reverse
is black or brown, and I
mean fascism, brother, not skin.)
His only worthy opponent
is the land alligator
I sometimes see coming
down the sand road. Then
I hide in the john
and give my own
basic product back
to the killing-ground.

To buy: 1. Dog
          2. Guns

To join: 1. Fish and Game Club
         2. Police and Auxiliary
         3. The Revolution

To conquer: 1. Alligator
            2. Loose bowels
            3. Sleep

ON WHEN McCARTHY WAS A WOLF AMONG
A NATION OF QUEER-QUEERS

At thirty, when the faiths give out,
and all the pleasures of light and air
go grey along with love, oh I began
to play the game: "Assumption of Faiths",
and took up spiritual hobbies. God,
sports, and country were not enough
for one American, so I became
a joiner lapsing from the faiths.
May whiskey, money, and analysis
survive me through committee days
and may the night yield sex,
in which release whole moments pass.

As for the rest, left-left politics
was out of law, so I read books and bit
my thumbnails to the quick
in false despair: I am still here.

CONFESSION OF HERESY

Once I demanded annihilation and frenzy.
I applauded the smiles of thieves and had
a passion for debris. Lost in the traffic
of argument, I appraised skilled assassins
and preached the slaughter of the pure,
but now I'm scared and only critical
of what I once proposed to wreck: I see
vandals at the monuments I hoped to save,
experts, who exceed in self my strong words,
and call themselves the business or the state.
They grow up in the rubble of our wreck,
kill with a purist's hatred of the strange,
and feed on death, until a liberal man
must blush like a rose for holding on to one,
turn grey, and learn to shout the slogans:
"Annihilation!", "Frenzy!", just to run
the gantlets of their streets in safety
from himself, them, or other enemies.

UNTITLED POEM

I used to enjoy the night-time
and foraged in it for my goods,
evils, money, laughs, girls and all.

I was the noise insiders heard at night.
They keyed themselves into the wards,
chambers, cylinders, and locks of bourgeois sleep.

But now that I stay indoors too at night,
I am afraid of off-lights in the sky,
of surface noise, and of my own eyes

looking at me in the black window-pane.
Oh I look out for dangers other than myself,
and rescue by and from the sounds and lights outside.

I DREAMED I GOT A LETTER FROM EZRA POUND

Oh I got jammed among the bodies as
they yelled away the air, enclosed. I slept
naked between two living pains. My chin-
bone plowed the floorboards as my talk,
all teeth, chewed at the salt ankle of
a raving man. I have been sent here
to commit the psychopaths to violence
and have succeeded. I have my disciples.

WAR DUTY

Through the left lashes of the left
corner of the left eye, a flicker: wings.
The right eye, blind in reserve
on the reverse slope of the nose,
reports nothing. The command
center of the brain commands: No
corroboration. Hold fire. No
retreat, no advance, no war, no peace
until it can be stated: "Dove
or avenging angel binocularly seen."

STENTOR AND MOURNING

Sunday was calm and airy
but artillery over the hill
made us too nervous to like it.
Some private tacked his tin
mirror to a palm tree and shaved,
using his helmet for a bowl
that would not hold
much water Monday night. I wondered,
stretched out in the while,
in the sleepy diarrhea of fear,
why soldiers fear remarks
more than a probable mutilation,
and swore myself someday,
after the important war,
to a rule of disobedience
as the bravest way. Nevertheless,
the captain's football voice,
bully as acne and athlete's foot,
commands as public law,
prussian as gossip or
the discipline of smiles;
just like when Hera rallied the Greeks
as they cried by their ships:
she yelled from Stentor's mouth
and they fought again,
not for Helen and souvenirs
or even the gods' graces, but
for Greek good opinion. Now,
after survivors' Friday,
in the short weekend of peace,
I hear that why we fight

is for a buddy's safety or
for vengeance for his death, but
I hold that most of us
nurture a fear in secret,
by and large, about our states'
power: some of us,
unknown in arms, can be
Patroklos in his onrush or
Akilles in his sulk
against the private feat
of doing as we god-damned please,
or charge a public hill
to an approved early death
under the national aegis.

ON VISITING A VETERANS HOSPITAL

Even if a man has been
chopped down to be
a basket case and has
gone mad with it, he
doesn't lack honor nonetheless.
After such actionless accidents,
honor adheres to those
who spend their subsequent lives
mindlessly singing of before.
So why not give the man a shot,
empty his bed-pan, or let him out
of the army and on to the street
to beg for women, money, and pleasure.

ON GOING UP TO SURGERY IN THE MORNING
AND IN FAVOR OF PAIN-KILLING DRUGS

The barber nurse has shaved off sensitive hair.
Another looks at the tip of her needle.
It sprouts a clean drop of ease. One
after the other, we all go up to surgery,
strapped to our pains but drugged. Time
becomes blood. It rises from the cuts upstairs.
So, human intervention in human forms
goes on to cure or kill the living flaws.
I envy everything outside the window except the stars.
They are too hot, too far away, and dying. They indicate
pre-operative concerns and mutilative traumas
afterwards. We all say, "We shall be changed,"
and will be, vanishing in a painful flash of star-time.
In the mean time, drugs could help the agonized.

DEATH'S CHICKEN, NAMED AMELIA

I used to be bothered by death,
a bird, who flapped for claw-
hold on my sick-room's window sill.
I prayed to the yellow beak
never to peck at the window pane,
and prayed to the ringing glass
never to shatter when it did.
It didn't, and I almost healed the breach
between my flesh and dreams
that scarlet fever burned through me
and went out sunning in the back yard,
recovered to a clucking friend,
death's chicken, named Amelia.
Oh she pecked grains to death in dirt
and kept an eye cocked at the sky
where I and the danger lay.
Because I fed her, she had flown
to unfamiliar heights for me,
and when she disappeared
in bad times, in depression soup,
her bones cracked in the milk facts
of my teeth. I ate her death for life,
and went on dreaming out of flesh, wise
with the wings of love sustaining me,
and beat her de-fleshed drum-sticks on my plate
in my heart's readiness for world war.

TWO COMMENTS ON
"DEATH'S CHICKEN, NAMED AMELIA"

I

It was a matter of life and death
for her to be exactly as she was,
while I lacked reason for the fear
that make me think a bird was death,
and called my appetite its cause.

II

That guilt was no catharsis:
I still fear my own death,
her death, and death's death.
"Death's death" means life;
once we kill off all life,
nothing can die, right?, so death's
dead, killers, brothers and sisters.

BOY AND EDUCATION

Going out naked in August fog
was swimming and the moon
was like a rolled-up worm.
If that was swimming what
was swimming in the moon-lake:
water of water, milk of earth, and moon-blood.

Oh he will winter seated
chalky as his standing marm.
How ocean's distillate
can salt a boy
and Education dust him.

A normal school would teach
    The Butterfly:
  Its Systematic Dusting
    Into Law
   and how it was
  a moonlight's worm
   a night before,
    but doesn't,
teaching the social system.

TEACHER'S LAMENT

The sidewalk says,
in chalk, that he
loves her. What a joke.

So fall is here
again and school
forces the issue: to sow

at harvest. It sits
the sexes side by side
to learn the mysteries

as if they could. Then
they can drive out
on first cold Friday nights

to learn their first delights,
pay later, and dream love.

TEACHER'S VACATION LAMENT IN THE COUNTRY

To have a toothache and no competent dentist,
poison ivy of the groin and an affair,
a sprained ankle in walking country,
and going broke vacationing — these
are just occasions for cocktail party humor.
What is decisively lousy is to be
out of whiskey on Labor Day
when the liquor stores are closed
and the merchants fly the flag for blood,
not solidarity, the labor movement, and stars,
while having to go back to town to teach
what, to whom, how, and why, on Tuesday.

CONVERSATION WITH A
DIRTY-MINDED LITTLE GIRL

What's a virgin?
    You are.
Is that good?
    Good and bad.
    Those joys and pains
    your singers
    sing about
    are real
    but never mind:
    you've bought
    their records and
    will add
    to them in time.

ON A PARTY

The children hung around
and played Monopoly, getting mad
at just a game while we
talked out with alcohol and hash
about the rising cost of love and death.
At least adults can stone themselves at play
and screw behind a lock at last before
an audience of children's wondering dreams,
while they themselves must fight themselves
asleep alone in sour propriety, sober in fear
of the night coming down on them
with futures of the talking night-wind.

UNTITLED POEM

What I remember most
about her is her clear eyes
and lips talking all
the time: no conversation,
no screwing. When I tell
her that I'll write a love
poem to her she says Great,
excuse me for a minute,
I have to go to the john.

Did you make the poem.
No.

A red leaf
fell in her hair
and got stuck in it
earlier in the day.

My heart rocked my body asleep that night
but I woke up sweating with terror anyhow
at four o'clock in the morning, for the usual reasons.

MORAL DREAM

A little girl in white, gold-haired,
came to my dream and brought a gift:
it was the doll of Christ. I was elect!
not by my virtú but by dreams equipped
to take the gift. Oh Gift-Taker, Sir
Equipment to the goddess Pedophilia,
she came to my bed in long gold hair,
and what I did with her I do not know
because I slept in sleep. When I awoke,
asleep, I found her head balled in the bone
crux of my elbow's calipers. She had
a dead man's face to measure: young
Hitler's, curdled in the flesh, with black
straight hair and two front teeth
knocked out: he was the dead doll of Christ.
I felt an instantaneous tree of ice
invade my nervous system and connect
dreams' dreams to an historical reality.
Thus, I expected subsequent atrocities
and woke for whiskey and an armed life.

ABSENT GOOD GIRL, LIFE OF MY MIND,

I'm alone in the house.
The wind is outside.
You're in my head.
We look out the window.
A crocus is opening visibly.
We forget dream-fucking you.
I go outside to smell it.
You are there in the flower.
You and the flower can never
know of my love for you two.

FOR A LOST GIRL

The skinny girl I never loved and lost, ah how
she pressed against me, how I pressed her so
she disappeared in me, ribs meshed into ribs,
prick into cunt, toes into toes to the heels.
She turned on our pelvic bones and settled in,
locked in my bones in itching sweetness. Then
she fell asleep, smiling. That's how I lost her.
She is the one I walk around with in the way
the marathon dancers used to do it: she
asleep in me, while I dance after a prize.
So when I hear a girl's voice in my mouth
or see another's eyelids on my eyes when I'm asleep,
it's her, so I come to her in losses of wet dreams
the wrong way, outward, not inward to herself.
It is by this love that I rationalize myself
to myself, in hopes of the death of first self-love.